I0458116

A HERETIC

WITHOUT

A HOME

poems by Megan Kemple

Copyright © 2025 Megan Kemple
Cover Design: Lane Hutchinson

ISBN: 978-1-968451-05-9

Published by Arcana Poetry Press.
P.O. Box 136 Montgomery, NY 12549
https://www.arcanapoetrypress.com

ARCANA
POETRY PRESS

All Rights Reserved.

No part of this book may be reproduced, stored, or transmitted in
any form or by any means (electronic, mechanical, photocopying,
recording, or otherwise) without prior written permission from the
publisher or the individual authors, except in the case of brief
quotations used in critical reviews or scholarly works.

For Grandaddy, Nana, & Uncle Dave

To the little girls that held it all in,
& the grown women who can't stop it spilling out.

CONTENTS

01. BLUE

05. FOR GOD SO LOVED THE SANDBOX

10. IN MY DREAMS, I'M ALWAYS HERE

12. DEPLOYMENT

15. RABID DOGS

17. PLASTIC FLOWERS

22. JUST GONE

26. MY UNCLE AND ME

36. GRANDADDY'S FUNERAL

39. DANDELIONS

BLUE

When a Soldier kills his wife...
and a Cop...
in my hometown
I wonder which color we will use to camouflage
this cover-up.

The answer is Blue,
to the tune of 22,000 car decal copies
of Trooper Davis' badge,
Blue Lines down the middle,
Blue Lines down black and white American flags,
Blue light bulbs handed out like free lunches
at the Elementary school,
High School boys in Blue uniforms
bussed like a chain gang to his funeral.

They send out a letter,
Report to your porches at the sound of the Fire Whistle,
form a Thin Blue Line, but keep silent.
A domestic between a Soldier and a spouse
is to be expected.
Poor Officer Davis died in the line of duty...
she just died like she was supposed to.

The Soldier had a hit list before High School,
the Judge sealed his records
and shipped him out.
When he couldn't buy a gun,
the government gave him one.
Now they have no idea how
he got his hands on an AK.

When I point this out,
a stranger tells me not to *bash the military*,
as if it's not still curdling in my blood.

When my sister
graduated from Warrant Officer school,
just like her Father,
the Commander said,
This job will rot your families from the inside out.

My Mother flashed back
to government laptops smashing against the wall, smelled the
whiskey-soaked hardwood,
felt his hands ripping her hair,
she said,
At least they know.

This town knows what a living ghost looks like,
the bruises they leave on loved ones when they detach from
their own skin.
When the werewolf gets stuck in beast mode,
we don't call them beasts, we call them
Red-Blooded American Heroes, Infallible Gods
no matter what they've done.

I wonder if the neighbors thanked him for his service
as he sprayed bullet holes all over their home
instead of someone else's.

They hold the Trooper's funeral at the gym on base,
embalm him in 100 proof Toxic Masculinity
and a funeral mask of Fake Patriotism,
and isn't that just like the Army?

To cover their sins in ceremony
and forget the civilian casualties?

They marched the Soldier,
barefoot and shirtless,
into the courtroom
like a Westworld robot
that needed rebooting,

A finely tuned killing machine
they like to call them,
but they must have forgotten his name…
call him *ticking time bomb*
instead of *active duty*
and we play Good Germans.
Bake apple pies to cover the stench,
sell the next generation
of military child brides
commemorative t-shirts
and teach them to
KEEP QUIET!

Thank the Soldier for his Service,
Thank the Trooper for his Sacrifice,

                              …and bury her in silence.

FOR GOD SO LOVED THE SANDBOX

For God so loved the world,
He gave His only begotten son.
John 3:16

For God so loved The Sandbox,
He gave His first family to the desert sun.

In this house,
Father is the proper name for God.

Our world—
His House,
His House,
His House.

His Rules-
or we'll all go to Hell tonight.
Sit up straight.
Clean it up, or I'll throw it away.
Do you want me to cut it off? Then stop crying.
YES WHAT?
YESSIR!
That's Chief God to you.

GPS tracker on His wife's car,
His wife WILL take His children to Church
while He sleeps off His hangover.

For God so loved Jack Daniels,
He *doesn't remember* what He's done.

Frankly,
that's a Family Readiness problem,
not His problem,
God never has problems,
God doesn't have a problem,
like I don't have a problem.

Just take the picture sweetie,
with the I Love You sign,
smile until it sets in permanently,
strive to be a Stepford Soldier's Wife.

Shut your mouth.
Stay strong for your sisters.
Stand straight,
straighter,
STRAIGHTER!

A morning-after silence,
a leaving for Iraq silence,
a drunk driving into the lake silence,
Silence.

Army brats don't cry.
Army brats don't question.
Army brats hide cuts under bracelets because
YOU WILL NOT EMBARRASS
THIS FAMILY LIKE THIS.

But let us go back to the beginning,

Once, God had a God who flew birds over Vietnam,
and that God had a God who flew birds over Korea,
and he married a woman whose God
performed in the Pacific Theatre,
and they gave birth to my God.

Once, my God picked a favorite plaything
and named her Eve,
taught her that pain was always her fault,
tricked her, tested her, traumatized her,
showed her God's will was unknowable.

Once, I prayed to God for hours
and was still too scared to sleep,
God pays the electric bill,
so when he says, *LIGHTS OUT*,
He means nightlights, too. I never understood
how anyone could sleep in the darkness
and silence of His House.

But back to the beginning,

God gave me life, and
God gave His life for me,
God would forget my name if it wasn't written
on an old phone bill,
God is too hard to talk to, so I blocked his number.

But let us go back,

His Daddy's Daddy's Whiskey
begat His Daddy's Whiskey,
which begat His Whiskey,
which begat His childrens' Whiskey,

and God's love begat the holes in hearts and walls,
and those holes begat new holes,
and the holes craved someone who would stay,

but they were holes, not healthy,
so they always left.

His love is leaving,
His love is *Don't you understand*
how gone I was for you?
His love is unopened Christmas presents,
and missed Toby Keith concerts,
and *I thought you were on a different continent.*

His addictions begat His love,
His love begat His mistresses,
His mistresses begat my love addiction,
my love addiction begat my sex addiction,

and my sister's love addiction begat her sons,
which He still hasn't seen
because His second wife begat him
a Replacement Son who He hasn't fucked up yet,

and His threats against a gay baby
begat my brother's terror,
and his terror begat my rage,
and my rage begat all the children I will never have,
who will watch God's name buried in the sand.

IN MY DREAMS, I'M ALWAYS HERE

Dad's favorite sport was hockey.
He spit the glass panes of the French door
out like teeth,
bloody and broken
on the living room floor.

I piqué through *Perfect Photo* frames,
split and sparkling shards
saying if I keep spinning,
I almost can't feel the glass grinding
into my mangled feet.

Spinning like his helicopter blades,
high as I can get,
Up! Up!
& as far away
from each other as possible.

I wanted to go to space camp
to fly higher than he ever could.
Better not to waste his precious money
on a girl who doesn't trust herself
or the government.

Better to dance
through the dark, dark house
which sits sinking,

decaying from the demons
we waltzed with for years.

Wallpaper still peeling like skin,
wood still next to the stove,
undisturbed by the anger interred
in the depths of the basement,
cracking our foundations.

I will not dye their camouflage pink,
glitter the gruesome

of gold star adjacent robots
with haunted hallway eyes.

Coaches always told me
I land like an elephant,

too loud and hard
for a wife as demure as my mother.

I scream
to anyone who will listen.

I don't believe in celebrating silence.

DEPLOYMENT

1. Take
Uniforms & Flight Suits—neatly rolled, patches sewn on
Underwear—government issued
Socks
Boots
Toothbrush / Toothpaste
Comb
Razor
Deodorant
Sunscreen—Death Valley strength
MRE's
Field Kit
Camelback
Chem Lights
Weapon—cleaned & ready to be assembled
Ammunition
Dog tags—2 sets
Under Armour
Kevlar Vest
Helmet—to catch the strays

2. Leave
the dog commands
unopened Christmas presents
the names of your children
your wife's vows
your mother's prayers
your father's guilt

mercy
safety
sanity
your soul

3. Report
firing every round, but no civilian casualties
6 dead friends, but no PTSD
hard landings, not helicopter crashes
unidentified resistance, not friendly fire
6 Soldier's Crosses, not 6 families
Classified Information, Not at Liberty to Discuss
I thought I saw a weapon,
couldn't find it in the rubble

4. Return
Stick to the shadows
Lord over whiskey island, bathe in its warm waters
No one gets clearance to your head
Paint murals of the desert
in the blood of your body count
Drink a beer for every buddy blown to bits
Forget your wife's name, forget your own name
Forget how to feel anything but strange pussy
Rename your children leeches,
apply yourself to peeling them off of you
Pull the quills of Fatherhood out of your skin
Exchange one family for a newer model

5. Drink
and drink
and drink
and drink
and drink
and drink
and drink
for freedom,
for glory,
for valor,
for a paycheck,
for a legacy

*Old soldiers never die, never die, never die, old soldiers never die,
they simply fade away*

RABID DOGS

Daddy,
you taught these hands to pray,
forced them together inside your fist,
taught me my place was on my knees.
These hands hold knives now,
and sharpen them in worship,
pray only for guns,
for retribution.
I want it,
need it like a purpose.
Grant me the weapon,
and I will give you such an assassin,
poisoned lips,
nails flecked in venom,
stilettos stocked with ammo.
Replace my bones with
those 3D printed guns Luigi made.
Make me over in your image.
Father, forgive me
for I found your DNA
twitching in my trigger finger.
This bloodline comes with an unholy body count,
the rapes, the beatings, the murders
on foreign soil and the backyard barbecue.
I hear their screams in my ears,
those screams are mine now, Daddy.

And so, no—
I have no remorse as I turn the gun on you.
It will be justice done,
You and all the You's like You—
rabid dogs on the hunt for whoever crosses your path.
It's time I put you down.

PLASTIC FLOWERS

My hands sink into his burial dirt trying to plant
the plastic flowers.
The hollowed-out holler
shuffles the dying past the dead,
like a line back in time
from the grave to his glory days
as an '80's football star.

                                  State champions.

Found the ring in the chest
Mamaw rarely opens
since her Mama died in '94—
holding locks of ghostly hair & baby teeth,
pictures of cars before they plowed into porches,
five grandchildren's preschool drawings,
four quilts her mother made by hand,
three Letterman jackets,
two of her brothers' watches,
one of her daddy's tobacco pipes,
& every birthday card her baby boy sent her
for 47 years.

                              There won't be a 48th.

Mountain People take care of their own.
Soon, at Granddaddy's,
there are five casseroles,
four prayer quilts,

three wooden crosses,
two ceramic angels,
& one windchime—

        hanging in a tree by the cemetery fence

which Uncle Trace & Grandaddy &

                Uncle Dave

built with their own hands,

        its lonesome echoes down the hill

to knock on their doors

        like he's still crying for help.

On Family Land he lays,
& on Family Land they will all stay,

              but I,

I am afraid of a backwoods burial,
terrified of nothing more than staying in one place.
I've been running from my accent
as long as I can remember,
but it shows up the minute
I hear my family on the other end of the line.

        When he called me,

a week before he shot himself, he said,

I read your book. Why are we like this?

I told him,
I have no more room for the feelings
of drunk and violent men,
and hung up.
Got into NYU,
tried to write a perfect life in concrete
with turnstiles of poetry,
where no one knew I had an accent,
or an addiction,
or six.
Where no one knew

                              I was poison.

Imagined myself a healer,
a drama therapist,
a good person.
That night I made a second call,
I told Grandaddy,

                    Drive up on the road.
                    Uncle Dave needs you.

& he said,

        Well, darlin', if he's got that bullshit in his head,
                    he's got that bullshit in his head.

By which he meant:

If he kills his cheating ex-wife,
he kills his cheating ex-wife.
Southern justice.

But Uncle Dave changed the play,
with five seconds
in the fourth quarter
he had three options:

                                   her, him, or the two of them.

At the last second

                                 he refused to pass the bullet

& as it touched down on his right temple,
I wonder if it sounded like

                         the deafening roar of a small town

southern football crowd at State's.
I bet it felt like the first time
you do a back handspring
on the track after they score—

                                     terrified,

giddy,

                         relieved you finally did it.

But plastic flowers
make a shitty

                                        Homecoming

bouquet.

JUST GONE

My Mamaw did not cry,
or look like she could,
when they told her my Uncle killed himself.

Simply said,
Well, that was my baby,
and lit a cigarette.

Went to the graveyard
to ask her mother's ghost
why her son forgot about her,

why his last words were,
Do you love me now?
to a wife that never did,

when his Momma
had always lived
and died for him.

Her mother had no answer,
just reached up from the grave
and pulled her daughter down for a kiss,

breaking her shoulder in the fall.
She did not cry,
or look like she could,

bruising creeping like kudzu down her arm
as she touched the yellow gray mold they used
to fill in her son's right temple.

Why did you do that,
you know I can't live without you.
she said matter-of-factly.

She did not cry,
or look like she could,
just told him a truth only the dead and dying know.

Another black curse sealed
to this macabre name.
I'll cry for you one day,

she said to
the face stitched back on after the autopsy.
And she did.

The next morning,
right before they lowered him into the ground,
a horrible howl as her soul cracked in half.

Two days later,
the strongest woman I know
could not feed herself,

or tell you the town where she has lived her entire life.
Congestive heart failure,
a body verging on sepsis,

every time they fixed one thing
another organ would go,
the doctors couldn't figure out what was wrong.

But she didn't cry,
or look like she could,
because my Mamaw was trying to die.

They say her dementia is caused by mini seizures,
but I know she leaves by choice,
goes somewhere it doesn't hurt so bad.

Her lungs churned out death rattles,
but the machines kept slapping the reaper's hand away.
I couldn't be the only one there thinking

we are robbing her of her death.
I told my Uncle, he made this mess.
If he's going to take her, too,

come take her,
because she had a hard life,
a backwoods mountain single mom

with three kids, two jobs,
and an abusive ex
kind of life,

and it just ain't right
to give her a hard death, too.
Or maybe what I'm saying is

don't let me die like this,
searching for precious words
that won't come.

Alone
in the most permanent sort of way.
A stranger to my own mind.

If the choice is his bullet,
or her brain,
I pick the bullet every time.

MY UNCLE AND ME

I come from Born Again Christian Backwoods.
Right.
So, we **don't drink,**
but my Uncle and I REALLY drink.

This Christmas, my Uncle Dave and I
fill White Claws into water bottles in the back bedroom
in preparation for 20/20
at Grandaddy and Grandma Brenda's house.

I ask him why we didn't do this together years ago,
he just winks and puts his finger to his lips.
Tonight's special is on Jim and Tammy Bakker,
disgraced 1980's televangelists.

They get to the rape charge against ol' Jimboy
and Grandma Brenda says,
Matthew 7:15: Beware of false prophets,
which come to you in sheep's clothing,

but inwardly they are ravening wolves.

I don't call this victim blaming.
God says many men will call His name
and He will reply "I never knew you."
I don't say God is an abusive boyfriend.

Grandaddy says *Now Megan,*
you've got two things in this world, and only two,
The Lord and your blood, in that order.
My Uncle smirks and chugs his Holy Water.

I swallow that and most of my identity in the silence.
We sneak outside to share a blunt,
laugh like I can't
when they spin that Old Time Religion.

When I put on a Sweet Submissive Southern Stepford
Soldier's Wife Smile—
a cowardly white kinda smile—
yellowing with age, rotted at the core.

Empty cavity of White Jesus
such a sore spot, I get lockjaw.
But thank 6-pound 8-ounce Darling Baby Jesus
for Uncle Dave and secret stashes

serving one more dose of silent protest.

I baptize myself in our Blood Curse,
Sap of the Split Trunk of our Family Tree.
It tastes like more peace
than I have ever found on my knees.

Once everyone else goes to bed, I break
as Jason Aldean echoes my Daddy's Garth Brooks,
All the cards are on the table, no ace left in the hole,
I'm much too young to feel this damn old.

My Uncle laughs at me for
being a weepy drunk,
at least he would if he were here, but
I put two red-blooded American coins over his eyes in March.

Once the mortician made sure no skin
had shifted during the ceremony;
an Old Country Celtic tradition,
just like someone did for His Grandaddy.

It was a good rebuild…
remarkable, actually,
how they filled in the hole from a 40-caliber bullet.
You could hardly tell it was wax.

You see,
the only time I ever held my Uncle's hand
was in his coffin.
We were never close in life.

My two Uncles got in a drunken brawl one Christmas,
and he didn't speak to the family for twenty years.
By the time he came back around,
I had long outrun my accent.

I only had one real conversation
with my Uncle Dave in all my life.
He called the night before I auditioned for NYU,
a week before he shot himself.

That night,
he was so far down the list
of people who would listen that
he called me.

Broke a lifetime of silence by slurring
I read your book. Why are we like this?
Twenty years makes no difference
when blood recognizes blood.

Mine froze.
I could have been talking to my Uncle or myself,
but even before I got into drama therapy school,
I knew enough to say, *Generational Trauma.*

The proper term is **Epigenetics**,
but that is a side point in semantics that amounts to
a Blood Curse exacerbated by environment,
poisonous fruit that begets poisonous fruit.

My Uncle and I are the nightshade
hidden in the Easter flowers.
My Grandaddy's Grandma taught
his Daddy to drink,

and His Daddy taught Grandaddy,
and Grandaddy taught His children,
and my Momma married a man like Her Daddy,
so I learned to drink like my Daddy.

And so, we have passed down the Good Lord
and a nature that defies Him;
anger, addiction,
ascension and Armageddon.

I'm so damn violent
He sobbed,
after finding His wife
with another man.

I, a woman,
conditioned to subvert physical outbursts
into slow strangle holds,
paused.

As my Mother's daughter,
I know a drunk man is a dangerous man.
Where is your wife? I asked,
afraid of the answer.

*I told her if she leaves this house
I'm burning it to the ground.*
Still alive,
a good sign.

For when violence comes quicker than patience,
a woman's time is always ticking.
He spilled all over me for half an hour
as I listened to him like every ex-boyfriend.

I conjured the nights
I whiskeyed my way
out of heartbreak—
through their suicide attempts

and bi-polar breakdowns,
getting kicked out of school,
and ending up in the hospital—
I pondered every time I snuck a drink.

But there comes a point
you can't be complicit
in whatever happens
next.

When I asked Grandaddy to go down there that night,
he said *Well, honey,*
if he's got that bullshit in his head,
he's got that bullshit in his head.

By which he meant,
if he's gonna kill her,
he's gonna kill her.
Like it had already happened.

For women who step outside the church,
like her, or me,
everyone is okay with killing the whore.
They didn't think he'd shoot himself.

I found the book I wrote on his dresser,
I sat in the way he knew the depth of my pain
from two thousand miles
and twenty years away.

I took a bullet from his nightstand,
identical to the one that shattered his skull,
dropped it in a bowl of marbles in the back bedroom.
Couldn't fly with it.

But I keep it close,
hold it knowing, despite everything,
I held back,
turned the car before the bricks,

dropped the knife before the bath.
The Feminist in me wishes
I could say that I reached out to her
when he shot himself in front of her,

asked if his blood got in her hair,
gave her the name of a good therapist,
invited her kids, who might be his, to lunch,
but that's not what happened.

Southern Scottish blood still runs hot,
and mountain people have always had their own desperate
kind of magic,
a creep in the dark that protects their clan.

Spells women carried in their aprons
cracked over the fire next to his grave,
as I bound her fate to his,
Dark Magic.

Blood Curse,
who am I in this?
The Addict, The Witch, The Whore, The Enabler,
both him and her.

The Dead and the dying,
the Cursing and the cursed.
My Uncle's watch ticks away
the moments I have left.

A seed interred in the dirt, my bloodline
is a debt to be paid.
Night don't get darker
than a Virginia graveyard.

Addiction is my Mother Tongue
and violence its accent.
Suicide could come
any Saturday night.

My fate is bound to his,
my blood is the only life
he has left.
I'll be damned if I don't use my magic.

GRANDADDY'S FUNERAL

How do I mourn a love as strong and steady
as the Appalachian Mountains?
As bright as a field of fireflies
and as dark as the holler at midnight?

How do I bury the only man who ever loved me
unconditionally and unapologetically
from the day I was born
to the day he died?

How do I rebuild on land that has been washed away?
Take a step forward when I'm drowning?
Know that I'll never sit at a table with you again
and still eat?

I didn't make it to you in time.
I didn't get to hold your hand
or say goodbye.
Not until you were in your casket.

But I know you were there,
because you put on
You're Gonna Go Far
as we pulled into the funeral home.

I made everyone get out of the car
so I could scream cry with you,
like I did at Uncle Dave's grave last year.
We both know you never got over his death.

It broke my heart the way your world got so small without
him. I'm afraid of how small my world is without you.
You know how scared I am to be still,
but I'm standing at your grave even in New York.

You weren't even in the ground yet
when the family split into factions.
Any hopes for reconciliation
died with you.

I waited there until everyone else left,
let them say their goodbyes and welcome you
to Heaven, even though they hadn't had a kind word
for you in fifteen years.

When we were alone,
I told you *I'm so sorry I wasn't there.*
I said, *Thank you for everything, I love you,*
and kissed your forehead.

And then I placed the coins over your eyes,
like I had for your son.
Like long ago an old man had for your Daddy.
Like you had asked me to.

But my sister couldn't let me grieve you
in my own way.
Couldn't let the magic of tradition
pollute the coffin of Christianity.

Everyone here has been scared of my power
since I was 13. They think I'm possessed by demons.
I guess she thought those coins were a one-way ticket
to Hell even Jesus couldn't save you from.

That is my biggest regret.
I let her make me swallow that
instead of flipping a table
like you would have told me to.

I let them make me feel small for the last time.
I have to do everything I said I would
because you told me I could do it.
I have to climb out of this.

Please show me how.

DANDELIONS

Things did not go as planned.
I stare into the emergency room ceiling tiles
full of black lines that look like
dandelion seeds exploding across the sky.
I do not cry,
just stare...
float with these wishes in the wind,
somewhere sunny and warm
and not a hospital bed.

Dandelions are wildflowers known
for their bright disposition,
golden petals that fall off one by one until they look
like they have lost everything.
When all the pretty things have fallen away
and they look like they have nothing left,
they do something unexpected.
Rather than wither and die,
they sprout a seed head, with up to 200 seeds per flower.
A whole dandelion plant can only produce ten flowers,
but those ten flowers release almost 2,000 seeds—
2,000 possibilities that each go on to make
2,000 more possibilities.
That's why we wish on them—
especially when things do not go as planned.

The nurse tells me we can stop if I need a break.
I ignore her,
thinking of all the possibilities in this white sterile sky,
of all the hope so many seeds could carry,
and how many of them would never bloom
into the dream the dreamer dreamt,
but they would bloom into a new flower to wish on,
into more possibilities.
A sky full of possibilities.

I am here because things did not go as planned
and so there was a possibility...
one I could not take care of long enough
to bring to fruition.
A possibility that was real but now isn't.
That, too, did not go as planned.
Now my reality is staring at a ceiling
of pretend possibilities
wishing none of this had ever happened.

I am lucky.
I live in New York.
I know this,
but every doctor and nurse is sure to remind me.
I just can't believe what this country is coming to
they say, and I agree.

The decision was easy if the process wasn't.

The world is on fire,
I'm already eight days late on my rent as is,
and my body can barely play host to myself,
much less anything else.
It's simply unrealistic to think that either of us
could survive that way.
This is the compassionate choice for both of us.

I've never been afraid to write anything,
but I'm afraid of this poem.
I'm not afraid of the honesty,
I'm afraid if I write this poem,
some ass backwards Christian nationalist
will find it while I'm down south
and I'll be charged for a crime
that is not a crime,
just a choice.

So I'll write about dandelions.
And possibilities...
that hang in the air for a brief period of time,
before falling to the ground unrealized.
See, even those seeds
give life to thousands of other seeds that sprout
into dreams that do come true.

Possibilities that become real
when the time is right

ACKNOWLEDGEMENTS

To the team at Undercurrent, for the original publication of FOR GOD SO LOVE THE SANDBOX in *Preposition: The Undercurrent Anthology*, 2021.

To the team at Milkweed Press, for the original publication of DANDELIONS in the *Milk Press Summer Issue*, 2023.

Special thanks to Jace, Sarah, Kathleen, Ashley, & Dave.

Megan Kemple (she/her) is a multidisciplinary writer, performer, and teaching artist thrilled to join the Arcana universe. Her work is a fusion of theatre and poetry, and she is equally comfortable on the page and on the stage. As a playwright, her plays "Where There's a Will" and "Tough Love" were produced as part of the 2025 Chain Theatre One-Act Festival Off-Broadway. As a poet, she has been published in Milk Press, The Drama Therapy Review, Preposition: the Undercurrent Anthology, & other publications. As a slam poet, she placed 3rd at the Rookie Slam at the National Poetry Slam 2017, & 3rd in the NUPIC Slam at NPS 2018, where her team placed in the top ten. Her first chapbook, *American Blasphemies,* was released through Ghost City Press (2017), and was staged as an immersive dance piece. She has an MA from NYU Steinhardt in Drama Therapy, and a BFA in Theatre Performance from Niagara University.

www.ingramcontent.com/pod-product-compliance
Lightning Source LLC
Chambersburg PA
CBHW020811130626
46554CB00006B/2385